Flip the Flaps

Things That Go

Anita Ganeri and Mark Bergin

KINGFISHER

NEW YORK

KINGFISHER
LONDON & NEW YORK

First published in hardback in 2010 by Kingfisher
This edition published in 2014 by Kingfisher

Distributed in the U.S. by Macmillan, 175 Fifth Ave., New York, NY 10010
Distributed in Canada by H.B. Fenn and Company Ltd., 34 Nixon Road, Bolton, Ontario L7E 1W2

Library of Congress Cataloging-in-Publication data has been applied for.

ISBN 978-0-7534-7133-3

Kingfisher books are available for special promotions and premiums. For details contact:
Special Markets Department, Macmillan, 175 Fifth Ave., New York, NY 10010.

For more information, please visit www.kingfisherpublications.com

Printed in China
1 3 5 7 9 8 6 4 2
1TR/1113/LFG/UG/128MA

Contents

On the road

There are many different things that go on the road, including cars, trucks, buses, and bikes. They have wheels to roll on, and most have engines to make them move.

car

tractor-trailer

1. An engine gives it the power to turn the wheels.

2. The rider pulls levers, and brakes rub against the wheels to slow them down.

3. Trucks need lots of wheels to spread out their heavy weight. Each wheel carries a part of the weight.

motorcycle

delivery van

bicycle

cab

truck with trailer removed

5

On the water

Ships and boats travel on the water. They carry people and cargo, or goods. They also do special jobs, such as fishing and rescuing people. Ships and boats are pushed along by engines, sails, or oars.

submarine at the surface

raising the sails

sailboat

6

1. The wind. The boat's crew sets up the sails to catch the wind, which pushes the boat along.

2. A submarine is a special kind of boat that goes underwater. People explore the seabed in submarines.

3. A hovercraft skims just above the water's surface. It is supported by a cushion of air.

A container ship carries metal boxes full of cargo.

A hovercraft carries passengers.

A fishing boat has nets to catch fish.

In the air

Things that fly through the air are called aircraft. Most aircraft have wings that keep them up in the air. Many aircraft also have engines that push them along.

nose of jet

small passenger jet

8

1. The wings use the air around them to push the plane up as it flies along.

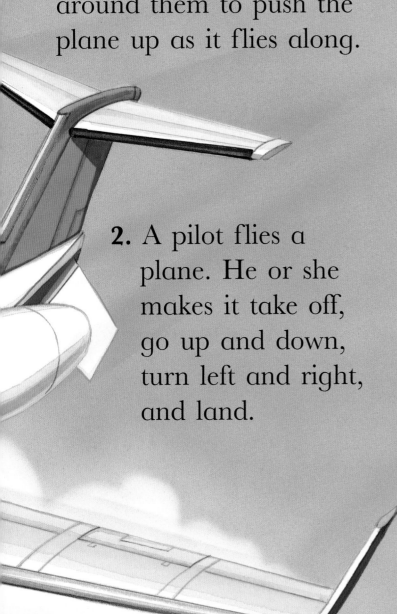

2. A pilot flies a plane. He or she makes it take off, go up and down, turn left and right, and land.

3. A rotor on the top of a helicopter spins very fast and pulls it up into the air.

propeller plane

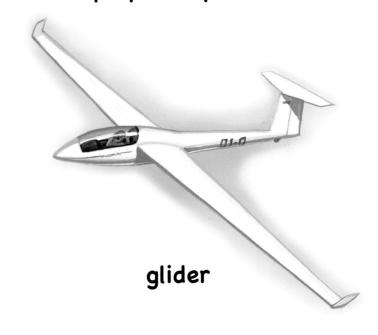

glider

helicopter

On the rails

Trains travel on railroad tracks. Their wheels roll along on metal rails. Trains are very heavy, so they need a lot of power to make them go.

tunnel

passenger train

10

1. Many trains have engines to turn the wheels. Others have electric motors.

A freight train carries cargo in cars.

2. Some trains travel through underground tunnels and even stop at stations under the ground.

A mountain train climbs up steep slopes.

3. The fastest trains are passenger express trains. They can go 186 miles per hour (300 kilometers per hour) or more!

A high-speed train carries passengers and sometimes cargo.

On a construction site

Machines on construction sites do lots of jobs. They help dig holes, move soil and rubble, and lift heavy loads. Big wheels or tracks stop them from sinking into the muddy ground.

crane lifting metal pipes

digger moving soil

1. Special machines called hydraulic rams move it. They push and pull like your muscles.

2. So that they can lift materials high up onto the tops of tall buildings.

3. A cement truck has a huge spinning drum. As it spins, it mixes the cement, sand, gravel, and water inside it to make concrete.

dump truck

bulldozer

cement truck

On the racetrack

Machines that go on a
racetrack are fast! Racecars
have powerful engines for
speed and wide tires for
gripping the track. It takes
a lot of skill and practice
to drive a car in a race.

racecar in
the pit

crew putting
on new tires

14

1. A Formula 1 racecar can go more than 215 miles per hour (350 kilometers per hour)—three times faster than a family car.

2. They wear a fireproof suit, shoes, and gloves, as well as a crash helmet to protect their head from bumps.

3. The rider leans far over, sometimes so far that his or her knee touches the ground!

stock car

race truck

racing motorcycle

Emergency!

Fire engines, ambulances, and police cars are called emergency vehicles. They help people in danger or difficulty. Their loud sirens warn people to get out of the way so they can get to where they are needed.

16

1. A fire engine carries ladders that firefighters use to climb into buildings. It also has hoses for spraying water onto flames.

2. So that people can see them coming and let them go past.

3. A lifeboat works at sea to rescue people.

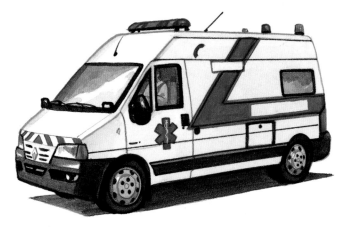

An ambulance carries sick and injured people to the hospital.

A police car takes police officers to emergencies.

A lifeboat helps people in trouble at sea.

17

Index

A
aircraft 8
ambulances 16, 17

B
bicycles 4, 5
boats 6, 7
bulldozers 13
buses 4

C
cars 4, 5, 14,
   15, 16
cement trucks 13
container ships 7
cranes 13

D
diggers 12, 13
dump trucks 13

E
emergency
   vehicles 16, 17

engines 4, 5, 6,
   8, 11, 14
express trains 11

F
fire engines 16, 17
freight trains 11

G
gliders 9

H
helicopters 9
hovercraft 7

L
lifeboats 17

M
motorcycles 5, 15

P
police cars 16, 17

R
racecars 14, 15

S
ships 6, 7
submarines 6, 7

T
trains 10, 11
trucks 4, 5, 15
tunnels 11

U
underground
   trains 11

V
vans 5

W
wagons 11

18

Flip the Flaps
Things That Go

Curious children can watch big diggers rumble, racecars roar, and hovercraft skim the waves with this interactive book. They will uncover the answers to questions about trains, trucks, planes, and other vehicles, and they'll delight in the unexpected scene changes as they flip the flaps.

Titles in the series:
ANIMAL HOMES · BABY ANIMALS · CREEPY-CRAWLIES
DINOSAURS · FARM ANIMALS · JUNGLE ANIMALS · PETS · PLANET EARTH
SEASHORE · THINGS THAT GO · WEATHER · WHALES AND DOLPHINS

KINGFISHER
KNOW | WONDER
www.kingfisherbooks.com

ISBN 978-0-7534-7133-3

$6.99 US
$7.99 CAN

50699

9 780753 471333

Things That Go

Flip the Flaps

Anita Ganeri and Mark Bergin